If This Heart Could Talk

AYMEN KHAN

For Alex,
If you could see me now.

'The worst part about anything that's self-destructive is that it's so intimate. You become so close with your addiction and illnesses, that leaving them behind is like killing the part of yourself that taught you how to survive.'

-L. L (via Fleurthorn)

'When you are,
not fed love on
a silver spoon,
you learn to lick it,
off knives.'

-Lauren Eden

Realistically, it's impossible to list all the names of those who have inspired me to write this collection of Poetry. This collection is just an accumulation of a very small amount of trauma. I've suffered with depression since I was around eleven, although, it feels like forever. Depression robbed me of everything. It was feeling nothing and everything all at once, all the time and there was no escape. Depression was a one-way street. This book has been the first good thing born from my depression. I know there will probably be more good things, but I've always been a cynic. I think that this book is a small fraction of my ugly truth. A demonstration of how a toxic home can change a person. The ugly, wonderful, murderous truth. We keep so much inside of us, pushing it down until it feels like nothing more than a small discomfort. We like to believe we are right. Like to believe we are the victims, the hurt, the wronged ones but sometimes, we're the villains. We're the villains of our own stories and maybe others too. Sometimes we're the selfish, toxic, narcissistic and desperate ones and for a long time, I didn't know how to live with that. Can we be a miracle and mistake at the same time? I was raised in a very toxic, sometimes abusive and emotionally violent home and It has shaped me into who I am today. I'm only my own friend when I need to be. I have to try harder than others to be empathetic, kind and supportive. A lot of my poetry in this collection and others focus on that person, born from a toxic family, and how that home has carved a darkness into her, and what a toxic home can do. Growing up in an unstable toxic home meant that I formed obsessive, desperate relationships with people I necessarily shouldn't have and now have an almost dangerous fear of abandonment. I wanted this book to accentuate that loss is crippling, whether we've lost ourselves or someone else. How we learn to live on after suffering ambiguous loss, how to be okay knowing someone's not dead, they're just choosing to be gone. This collection explores the boundaries of human obsession and how far we're willing to go to keep those we love.

I think about you, you know.
It's like the day you left, I stopped loving all together.
You turned me into poison.
How sad that I have become the same bitter and resentful
person I used to detest all those years ago.
-A

What I wanted to preserve most were the moments as they were happening. The moments that seeped into my bones like tar and bound me to edge of madness. The ones that lulled me into a dreamless sleep, filled with the sudden awareness of passing time. I am trying to swallow down thick chunks of grief and regret, only I am choking. You are the past I am ceaselessly borne back into. Filled with familiarity, dangerously aware of the rules, breaking them anyway. I would keep them on a film reel that would play constantly and never fade. You are a shimmer I see everywhere. The outline of your face floats with me everywhere I go. All I have left are fragments of moments, slipping from my memory. Have your eyes always been that blue? I have let my pride nurse me into fakeness. Pride carries me high, through the broken glass, all the way up to the very top. When the simple truth is that I had my chance and I let it go. I watched it sail out of sight and now, all these years later I am searching for it. Now I understand the magnitude of my silence that day. I will have to live a lifetime without you.

Remember when you said you'd always forgive me? You speak.

I'm scared to look at you, although my gut already knows. *You should never have trusted him. You should never have trusted him.*

Again.

You spill all your crimes and all I can do is look at you. I heard somewhere that we keep forgiving people until we stop loving them. All I can think is '*please don't let it be true.*'

Remember when you said you'd always forgive me? I need you to live up to that promise.

-A

Your girlfriend is pregnant,

due in October,

I have not thought about you in so long and now all I can think about, is you, and your future child.

Will they have your eyes? maybe your bluntness. maybe they will be kind, something you learned how to be the hard way.

look at me, pretending like I know you. like I have ever known you.

they will be half of you and half of a stranger,

my gut tells me it is going to be a girl,

I hope I am right, maybe then you will realise that what you did was painful and wrong,

maybe you will realise that there were gentler, kinder ways to do it,

You were my first real love, unrequited though it was, it was love all the same.

Unrequited love is a death sentence, there are no boundaries, one can slip so easily into obsession, the fine line is blurred.

I understand now that love and hate are the same emotion, the same coin, just opposite sides.

I loved you, I still do. You are familiar to me.

The pain of loving you and not being loved back is so familiar and comforting yet painful,

It is why I have never got over you, not fully anyway, everything I know about love has been born from you,

from wading in the depths of what ifs,

I am happy for you, I think,

These days, I am learning to be happy for others and not bitter.

that was supposed to be my baby, you were supposed to love me, and if you could not,

If the idea of loving me was so abhorrent,

You could have had the decency to be gentle about it, instead of violent and hurtful,

Our encounters from high school are burnt into my eyelids,

I am over you, in the sense that the pressure on my chest has lessened over time,

the aching has lulled to an occasional pang,

if I am being honest, happy endings look good on you, you deserve the happily ever after you are getting,

I have let you go, unshackled you from the hate, the expectations, the past,

I hope your child is you, through and through,

Is this it? the part where I set us both free,

I hope you think of me sometimes, on the nights where the past does not let you exist anywhere other than within itself.

The grass is only green where we water it.
I used all my water on you. Can't you see?
I'm an empty watering can.
Stop pretending there's water in me when there is not.
-A

Turns out, even love is not enough.

-A

I am forgetting fragments of you.
They are falling everywhere.
I am scared to move in case I shatter them.
How do I fix this?
-A

It is okay to love them both.
I did.
-A

We will all be held accountable for our crimes.
So, fear not, this is what nature has promised.
-A

Someone always has to love more,
and I am sorry it had to be you,
-A

You made my eyes burn.
I guess I know why they say love makes people blind.
-A

You tasted bitter,
and scalding,
and rich.
You were momentarily intoxicating.
How could I have ever stopped myself from absorbing you.
-A

You set fire to us.
Everything smells of what we could have been.
We were destined to be the end of one another.
-A

If lying here, soaked in moonlight.
Is the closest I will ever get to emancipation,
I don't mind.
-A

I can't help touching your body.
I don't mind the cold, it's home. Comforting and smooth.
I don't even mind that my hands come away bloody and cut.
There's always a price to pay for people like you.
I don't mind paying with my soul.
I love you.
I was always yours to abuse and stitch back up.
-A

I dreamt about you.
Waking up was a hard blow.
It knocked the breath out of me, even harder than on the day you left.
You slip from my thoughts but never from my memory.
I keep you hidden, in a small fold in my heart, yet there is never room for anyone else.
Fear and pride held my voice hostage all those years ago.
I loved you.
You were probably the only one I loved.
My skin crawls at the regret,
If you ever come across these poems and wonder who they're for.
They are for you. Every single word is for you.
-A

You took everything you could.
All you did was take and take.
Loving you was expensive.
-A

The drive back down is a real-life metaphor,
Memory lane. Nostalgia. Bittersweet. Anger.
I turn my face the other way when we pass *that street.*
My sister stares at it, talking about how wonderful it was
there,
All I see is pain, ten years, never being good enough.
Everyone quietens when I say that it was everything never
meant for us,
They don't know that sometimes I drive to *that street,* and
park outside *that house,*
Trying to forgive and forget. Trying to find some good in
those walls,
Trying to find the love in those blood-soaked walls,
sometimes I'm there,
The forgiveness tickles my fingertips, I don't grasp it,
They don't deserve to forget. I'll come back tomorrow.
-A

I have been searching for you, quietly,
In coffee shops and malls and parks,
In supermarkets and parties and parking lots,
I stand on my tip toes scanning the abyss of people,
Hoping to find one with eyes like yours,
And a tattoo like yours,
I am always wading through this sea of people,
In search of you,
And when I find one that resembles you enough,
The panic rises in my throat and hope kisses my cheek,
Only to strangle me, when I realize they can't be you,
Tell me you're looking for me too,
Tell me that this isn't all for nothing.
Tell me that I'm not drowning in vain.
-A

We have always struggled to see the fine line that divides obsession from love. I want you to choose me, every time, even if it hurts you, even if you lose everything. I love you, but we keep walking this line between a minute and a lifetime and I want you in both. What do you mean, I can't be with you all the time? Rejection spears me and I feel overwhelmed with hate and fury for you. When you leave, an all-consuming, transcendent emptiness fills me. You scoop everything from within me when you leave and every time you try to refill me, there's less and less room for my humanity to fit. We are divine together; addicted to each other. When was the last time our fights didn't end up bloody? We love without reason, in spite of, regardless of. I am stupid and contagious. Can't you see? I'm dancing with my hands tied on this fine line and we've slipped so far into obsession that I'm not sure I want us to come out. you come to me and scream naked truths about me, about the hold I have, the spiteful tone I use, the words I use to stab others, the way I take advantage of what others feel for me and manipulate them into pleasing me. And when there's not a single naked truth left to be spilled, you force me to be normal. You force me to behave like it never happened. I hate *her* too, but you already know that. The only reason you married her was to spite me. I hate her even though we're exactly the same, it's why you can't pick between us. You want us both. Everyone tells us not to get involved with married men, but I was your muse long before you were mine. I'm not foolish, I know you won't leave her. But I know you won't leave me either. We're bound at the core so tightly that we have merged into one soul. We are threaded together with thorns and roses. We are one. You are within me and I in you. When did it slip from love into obsession? You ask me what game I'm playing. There's no game, not this time, not with you. This time, I'm playing for keeps. There's no rules. We can be what we want together. We can elude her, hide from her, float silently between these walls. Paint these walls with our story. We both know we will leave each other bloody with the shame of being in love and used, but there's still time, isn't there? There's still time to pretend that we're meant for each other. There's still time to pretend that what we're doing is right and justified because we're in love. There's still time to pretend that this blood and these scars are not from one another, but from past lovers, there's still time to pretend that we haven't mistook violence for passion. There's still time.

-A

I am an elite poison.
I have been weaned on poison my entire life,
So, is it really surprising when I say I find comfort in maltreatment?
A potent, syrupy, infectious poison,
Indeed, that is what it is, a toxic home,
It seeps into my bones, coats my mind,
The lies are like poison, the truths no less,
The smooth poison has eroded my heart, closed it off,
Part of it only pumps the poison throughout the body,
I don't have the energy to drain the poison,
Everyone needs to hurt the way I hurt,
Astronomically, dangerously, constantly.
They need to hurt and hurt and hurt,
Until they shrivel up, becoming hollowed out caves,
Robbed of humanity and purpose,
Daddy is so proud,
I am an elite poison, the most lethal of them all,
He admires that, what he has created,
A bitter, vicious woman.
-A

I like dancing with the devil.
He pretends that he won't kill me,
and I pretend that he'll save me.
It's strange, the devil looks exactly like you.
-A

We drunk text each other,
Even in our worst moments,
I always come back to you.
-A

You were the apple of my eye baby, red and loud and passionate.
But my god,
My god did you have a rotten core.
-A

Even the brightest stars would burn out before we did.
-A

Even the most powerful of witches could not save you
from my love spell.
Our anatomy was magic.
-A

How foolish was I to have built my walls so high?
I could not break them down, even if I tried.
-A

If I would have known that loving you,
meant losing myself,
I would have walked away that spring evening I met you.
-A

Staying silent that day was the greatest miscarriage of justice,
Our love story was always full of miscarriages.
-A

In 10 years, it won't matter how much money we had,
Or how many designer clothes we owned,
Or how drunk we got on the weekends.
What will matter, is what we felt,
and everything we never did about it.
-A

We both knew I was the devil.

A nightmare dressed like a daydream.

I was full of fire and you had a paper heart.

I had already claimed so many souls.

You begin to lose count after that many.

But you. You were the kind of soul I desperately needed to have.

Just you.

How did you unveil me so quickly? A worthy opponent you were indeed.

Did nobody tell you that you could never win?

Oh, my sweet, sweet angel, there is no better player, than someone who has nothing to lose.

-A

You told me once that you liked red,
So naturally,
I used all my blood to paint the walls for you,
And all you could say was *it's not the right shade of red*,
I should have known I would be the one left empty and
abused.

-A

Baby,
We were the perfect recipe for disaster.
-A

When the silence starts to drown me,
you're never there to rescue me.
I'm deluded, or perhaps I've never seen everything clearer.
I need someone to tell me that it's okay if I stopped loving
you,
Especially before I should've.
Oh, if these walls could talk.
-A

I remember that day so well.
My hands were stained red with blood.
I'm still not sure if it was yours or mine.
Our throats were coarse from the yelling.
Selfish.
Impulsive.
Angry.
What is it that we gave up?
You blew the cigarette smoke in my face,
and slammed the door on your way out.
So, I sat there, in another world,
with my dignity in shreds, wondering,
if I loved you too much, or if I didn't love you.
enough.
-A

The what ifs are mocking.
They taunt me with wishful fantasies,
how that one moment of silence is rippling into
an eternity of regret.
-A

Everyone knows I have daddy issues.
daddy's always give daughters issues.
fathers are meant to be emotionally eternal,
mine only gave me eternal suffering.
I am still trying to pick the pieces up.
maybe he was always like this.
maybe the good times were never good, but a fabricated
play of happy family.
which version of him did I love?
-A

You will always be the love story I tell my children,
when I want them to know what love is not.
-A

I am so defensive when it comes to you,
despite what you did.
I am fast to preserve your dignity,
when all you did was ruin mine.
-A

I try to force myself to fall in love with people that
resemble you,
but then the light illuminates them in all its glory, and I
finally see,
they could never be you.

-A

I never truly understood how radioactive you were,
you glowed brightest at night,
you were killing me slowly,
I can still feel the toxicity pulsing out from you,
I wonder how many more souls you claimed,
I am still emitting your frequency.

-A

How can I say goodbye to my very soul?
I always knew this day would come,
after all, he was only ever meant for greater things.
-A

Why did you treat me like I was some language class?
ho bisogno di una risposta.
you reached in and plucked the last shred of humanity,
from my soul.
I cannot bring myself to comprehend.
I cannot.
-A

Best friends are the people you go to for everything,
they are your home team, sidekick, partner in crime,
soulmate.
you were all those things to me.
the only source of light in a world of darkness,
and when the universe finally collapsed,
I realized your love for me was conditional.
you never understood that presence is not needed.
to preserve intimacy and loyalty.
you're not who I thought you were.
-A

My hardened brown eyes search for ones that hold the
same understanding,
as yours did.
nobody is enough.
I trail hundreds of women, hoping to find one like you.
someone who possesses your compassion,
empathy, and soothing energy.
I come up empty every time,
I should've realized by now,
not everyone can be all kinds of epic.
-A

I try to fill the void in me with every man I meet.
I lure them into my lair and erase the memories for a sweet
while.
these men are fools, we are in sync physically, but my mind
wanders.
I see your eyes in theirs.
I draw your tattoo on their forearms, they don't complain.
I am an enigma, and they can't wait to figure me out.
for a moment, I lapse back into the past that is you.
these are the kinds of men who love enigmas,
until they find one, they can't crack.
but I don't mind their anger, it feels like home.
oh baby, can't you see? I don't want to hurt them,
but I will if I must.
I will if it brings me a slice of you.
I might be obsessed with you.
-A

I am renegading. levitating. soaring.
The sky is candy floss, and the world looks like,
I'm staring at it through a fun house mirror.
Just one more.
the sheets are white with specks of blood, I'm a pin
cushion.
the look on my mom's face is frightening, malicious almost,
just one more. just one more.
-A

I sang you sweet melodies,
you listened, enchanted.
I was a siren, and you were a fool.
you were always a fool in love.
I was toxic and damaged, with a hell of a lot of daddy
issues.
I am sorry I used you, I did not know what else to do,
with someone as a giving as you.
-A

Everything is ablaze.
The buildings scream out.
Nature desperately tries to preserve herself.
Souls are crying, everything is so dense.
One final epic showdown.
And right at the center of it all, are us.
You and me.
The haunting blue melodies of the dying, combined.
with our heartbeats in sync, come together to perform,
one last orchestra.
You step forward to take my hand and we waltz,
A broken waltz,
The smoke is so thick, we dance fast.
Everything is racing to the climax, I'm spinning so fast,
Your face distorts into another.
Slowing down makes you dizzy and I'm,
Choking now. Oxygen has deserted me.
I turn around gasping and catch sight of the Capitol
building ablaze,
She falls and I fall with her.
This is the end. We should've listened to her, I whisper.
This is her swan song.
-A

I was devastating. Titanically devastating.
I was epically, deliciously, revolutionarily devastating.
I devastated you and her and them.
but you devastated me also, can you tell?
We were a show.
-A

I lie in his bed at 2:47, embraced by the darkness.
I don't know his name; I couldn't tell you to this day.
the room is deliciously cold.
his arm traps me next to him, I don't try to move it.
I'm bored, oh I'm so bored.
he thinks we would make luxurious lovers; I don't argue.
he doesn't know.
I deleted your number out of anger, yet I find myself,
absentmindedly dialing it.
'hey', your voice is thick with sleep,
you don't say anything, you know it's me.
you mumble your hotel room number and end the call.
I don't feel happy, or excited, or even sad,
I feel relieved, even after my constant infidelity,
you love me enough to keep me. I feel like I'm going
home.
I peel away the strangers' arm and climb out the window,
and jump the story. It doesn't hurt.
the cool Parisian air caresses my face as I stick my,
head out the cab.
I find you 'asleep', so still and serene, you look dead.
I know you're awake, you never mastered the art of
pretending.
I strip down and get in the warm bed. You look so
beautiful,
an angel, the man and the monster.
you're a fool too. You love me too much and I don't love
you enough.

there will be no questions the next day, there never are.
you know me by now. I can't stick with one person for too
long.
but perhaps it does not matter, I could fuck all the men in,
the world, but I would always come home to you.
we all return home.
-A

I wake up excited, regardless of what is happening. Today is my 18th birthday.

I'm celebrating 18 years on this planet. My silver helium balloons are waving proudly from behind the sofa.

I change into a regular outfit and the calls start to come in. Happy Birthday! says mom, says everyone. Everyone but you. I don't think anything of it at this point. Even though it's almost late afternoon for you. Maybe he's busy. Yeah, he's just busy. He'll call. He has to.

We cut the cake, have presents but you still haven't called and now I'm getting nervous.

Has he forgotten? Is this because he's angry with us all? Mom tells me to forget it, to swallow the lump in my throat and smile.

It's my birthday. I can't shake the feeling of betrayal. It's threatening to spill out.

Everyone knows what happens when I spill over.

My phone dings, it's a WhatsApp notification.

An automated Facebook video wishing me a happy birthday, sent by you.

A small 2 second pre-made Facebook video. No caption. Nothing.

It feels like a slap in the face. You already stabbed us but now you twisted the knife.

I don't spill. I bury it. I bury it so fast and so far, down that it becomes a part of me.

A part of my worth.

I had a realization that day, a beautiful one too.

You taught me that I shouldn't and couldn't trust anyone.

After all, if my father could do me like this, anyone could.

You played the guitar. A sweet melody. Sometimes a deafening beat. I couldn't ever decide which one you were. The lighthouse or the storm. Maybe both. The moon illuminated me as I looked straight at you. Infatuated by your beauty. Why did it have to be you? You asked if I wanted to see it. I breathed the answer. my hands itched to reach out and graze your sand-stained skin. The ink swirled around your skin, absorbing it, rapidly chasing the veins. How can a room so big, seem so small with the right person? how can a heart so big become so small by the absence of the right person? how can I still love you, after all this time? How can I still love?

-A

You have always been soft. cloud like soft. sensitive too. You were always so intimate with words, even though we were thousands of miles apart. You hated being deemed a savior. Anything other than ordinary. you wanted to bake me banana bread and sit on the floor and talk. you wanted to go to Paris and walk the streets. You wanted me to reach my peace picture. How did you not realize? You were my peace picture.

-A

You're all I've ever known. I opened my eyes, and you were there, always.

I realize now that I am recklessly possessive over you. You are half of my soul.

I love you the most, so why am I exhausted? I cannot leave you, you hurt me, yet I am always the one apologizing. It is the fear that speaks for me, apologizes on my behalf. I cannot imagine an existence in which you are not the center. Everyone tells me to leave you, that I have a voice and my self-worth is not dictated by my interactions with you. They might be right, but I'm scared. I'm so scared of having to live without you. Everyone I have ever known has hurt me; I don't need to tell you that. So even when you start spitting ugly truths about me and I get out of control, I forgive you in the moment, as you are hurting me, because surely to die a little more inside is better than losing you. I would've cut my heart out and let you break it if you asked. I don't have it in myself to go with grace, I don't have it in me to go at all. Are you hearing me? I'm sorry is what I'm trying to say. I'm sorry that I love you too much. Let's forget the fires, the hurt, the guilt sick love, can we just forget it all. Your silence is making me want to end it all. I don't want to be here if you don't want me anymore. do you even love me anymore? did you ever love me? I'm not sure of anything anymore.

the slanted sheen of the winter sun falls directly into his eyes, or his eyes are pulsing out the sheen? in this moment, it's impossible to tell. I can't break his gaze, it's a trance. A plan. A deviously sweet plan to mesmerize me and I fall for it. His skin is mine. I'm not breathing. Breathing is not happening. he is inside my mind, my heart. his words trigger an orchestra of feelings I don't recognize. *it doesn't have to be this way* he whispers.

his hands push down on my shoulders, the fire is spreading so fast inside him, I can feel the heat of it on my face. Vicious flames are born, die, and reborn. His eyes are a movie I cannot stop watching.

I love you he says in a way that tells me he doesn't. desperate. He knows what I'm thinking. he has delved deep into the archives that harbor every exquisite detail I have ever seen. he presses pause and start and delete. rewind. always rewinding. his face is wet, and it is then that I see it. There is something in his eyes. An urgency. A desperation unlike any other. Another version of him threatening to spill. In there he is every age he has ever been. Every age I will ever know him.

yes, I stumble out. my voice is not my own. I should be screaming *no no no*. He presses into my body, relieved.

what have I done?

I held on for so long because I thought that nobody else would love me. I figured it was better to be loved a little and abusively than not at all. I pretended that your words could plaster my cracks so smooth that they wouldn't be visible anymore. I could clean myself up, breathe a little deeper and submit myself to you. After all, you loved me. I laughed a little louder and glowed a little brighter. But you never noticed. Did nobody tell you? A star shines its brightest in the moments before it dies.

-A

The boundaries between the fields in front of me spell out a distorted 'A.'

They probably don't. They probably don't spell out anything at all, but it's easier to believe they spell out your name than nothing at all.

You've colored everything in you. I can't see a damn thing without sifting through the memory of you. We burned out a long time ago, yet the memory of you still ignites wildfires in my heart, in everything. You have power over me, like you did before, like you do now. I just need to work out if it's strong enough to hold me forever.

-A

And do you know what the most tragic part of this all is? I saw God in you.

-A

It's snowing as I write this. It's slow now, but I know it'll become aggressive. It's sporadic. It's strange, snow causes so many obstacles. Road closures, accidents, cabin fever, cold, and yet every time it happens, we're all mesmerized by it. It reminds me of you. No matter how much you hurt me, tried to block me from escaping, sliced me open and caved me empty, I'll drop everything to chase you if you ever came back. I'd leave the warm light and blindly follow you into the depths of hell. Always.

-A

do you believe in fate? you ask as we walk up the treacherous hill, breaths making love in the air. I say I believe we make our own fate. I'm talking about some movie, but I can't hear myself. I'm speaking a foreign language I don't understand. I turn to look at where you should be, only darkness greets me. I look further up and see the moon, spherically glowing. *oh, it's only you, moon,* I whisper as my eyes fill. The moon says nothing, it knows better. god how can silence be this loud.

-A

Azlan, God, writing your name is so difficult. What I am about to write is even harder. This is goodbye, although you don't know it yet. I actually just spoke to you on the phone before I started writing this, you said you were having pizza on the weekend. How innocent, you have always been so food obsessed. Whilst I am writing this, I am trying to imagine your face, the face that will open this letter, many years from today. You are a chatterbox, a leap of faith, a curious cat, so I already know that my death and absence will raise questions, but you are just three years old so you will most likely have no memory of me, all the time we spent together, all the McDonalds trips and food trips and water fights and angry faces that are just cute. And the saddest thing of all is that you will never remember how much I loved you. The main purpose of this letter is to remind you that I loved you. I love you so much, you were the next best thing after your sister. If only I could show you. You were the only person on the planet I would have sold my soul for a million times over and over again, Depression is a silent but deadly killer. I really do not know what the family has told you in terms of my death. It was a suicide. I was in so much pain and anguish that death was the only thing that could relieve me of it. People and their love stopped meaning anything because the pain was just too severe. I did this *because* I loved you, it might not look that way, but I promise you gulu, everything I do is for you. When you were born, I did not go to see you at the hospital. I was brimming with jealousy, I was angry, scared that you would replace me. After a while, I completely fell in love with you. My entire life revolved around you. I could hardly go a day without seeing you. I think maybe God sent you into my life at a time where I was exceptionally lost. A time where I lacked purpose, you gave me purpose. You were all the reasons to stay alive, packed into one 3-year-old body. I know you do not remember me; I am merely a stranger to you now. But once upon a time, you were the only reason I was alive. I know you are meant for great, epic and beautiful things. I have no doubt that you will make me proud, I am already so proud of you, Azlan. I love you. I have never ever stopped loving you. Always beside you.

I find you ten years from now, In the most unsuspected of places, absentmindedly fingering the books on the shelf, I can't quite believe it at first, I look away then look again, you're still there, which means this isn't a dream, A little trick you taught me a lifetime ago, so many words threaten to spill from me, but what could I say that would be good enough? What reason could you have for not finding me all these years? I have sailed by all these years with half swallowed words, and empty gazes and a wallet photo, with hollowed hearts and bleeding wrists, you were my medicine, Filing the pain away to a dull ache, you turn around and look straight through me, It's me, I want to scream, It's me! The one you swore you would find, I want to tell you how once upon a time, I lived and breathed and existed for you, only you, I caved and bled and burnt just for you, But I'm just as cowardly as I was all those years ago, So, I let you go, because I have always wanted you to be happy a little more than I have loved you, And I have, I have loved you, I have always loved you.

-A

I love you too much. You're always my priority. I couldn't leave you, even if I wanted to and I think you know that. You know it so well it's why you do this to me. Do so much without doing anything at all. I'm slipping under, there's no fight left in me. Did you win? It will be worth it if you have won.

-A

Oh baby, do not go parading around what you took from me. when your friends ask, do not narcissistically show them all the unique, exquisite parts you have of me. you only took what I wanted to you to take.

-A

I glance over to the couch; my eyes are full. Your mirage tells me to let it go and I don't dare move. I won't cry. I won't cry. You tell me I'm beautiful. I mumble '*obviously not enough to make you stay*' you sigh, we've gone through this a million times. I wipe my eyes and stare in the direction of the couch, ready to apologize but you have disappeared. You'll be back. I'd rather have your mirage than nothing at all.

-A

I watch you shake out of fear when he yells your name. You don't understand but you do. Damn that Cinderella keyring. What will he use this time? the sobs are breath stealing and come in waves. I can still feel the stinging on my face. I want to reach out and pluck you out of it. The fear is so abhorrent you wee yourself; this makes him even more furious. Can't you do anything right? he calls you downstairs after it has been done. he says he is so sorry; he asks to see the places where he has hurt you and the marks bleed red. he gets upset and your heart lurches. It's okay, it's my fault dad, I'm sorry dad. He tells you that your good kid but need discipline, he loves you that's why he hurts you. I watch the girl in front of me forget the abuse and hug her father. It does not matter that a few moments ago he was the monster, he is the man now and it is all that matters.

-A

There is a place between our worlds, an entire universe with stars and galaxies and unsaid words, I hope you find a way to get there one day. I wander the space looking for remnants of you. I'm building a castle with the bricks you threw at me; we can live there together. when you find your way, I'll be waiting here.

-A

The snow cushioned the blow when I surrendered myself. I tried to look upside down and I swear I was gazing into another world. My breath danced in the air, creating pretty pictures. The aqua sky kissed the yellow light and enveloped the sound. *Is this what dying feels like?* You're a movie that I keep watching. You flash in front of my eyes. the way you laughed, got embarrassed when your voice broke, football, pouring rain and math books, guitar tattoos and phone calls. Snow angels and golfs. Marathons and bleeding nipples, icy icy blue eyes. I get up and I'm in a surreal snow globe. The light touches the surface and you're here. My eyes well up and I can hardly run to you fast enough, the light is blinding, and the snow is crisp and you're a mirage. You're a mirage. You're always a mirage. I catch sight of the ground and it's then that I see it, a perfectly made snow angel right next to my messy one. *'mine's still better'* I yell to your face in the sky as my tears freeze. You were always the angel.

-A

This betrayal hurts more than dads, I know you're going to be fine without me because you always were, and I guess it doesn't matter anymore. I forgive you always because I love you, even if you don't. I feel dizzy with realization and hate. I love you S, but I hate you too much right now. I hate how you hurt me. But that's just it isn't it? Even when I hate you, I love you too much. I cared too much, and you didn't care enough.

-A

I have always struggled with forgiveness. Especially forgiving you, dad. What you did was a movie turned nightmare, Only I was awake all this time. I forgive you for it all. All the before stuff, anyway, Sometimes I doubt that forgiveness, but it's there. Sometimes, the urge to snatch that forgiveness back is so strong, But I can't take it back, even when I want to, you cannot give me back ten years, and even if you could, I would not want them anyway; they would not erase what you did. I am not sure if I love you all the way yet, but perhaps the beauty of this, is that I don't have to. I forgive you, not because you deserve forgiveness, because you don't. I forgive you because I deserve emancipation.

-A

You're up to your old tricks again and this time, I don't get to be shocked or angry or hurt. I don't get to blame anyone but myself. I gave you another chance. A chance you begged and cried for. A chance you swore you would never waste and here we are, only one year later. Why do you keep doing this, dad? I shouldn't have trusted you or believed you. A part of me feels sorry for you, you can't help who you are. You can't help that this is all you were taught. An apple tree will only ever grow apples, never mangos. I can't do this anymore. I am sorry that you have forced me to hate you, when all I wanted to do was love you, but actions speak louder than words and your actions have left wounds too bloody and memories too sharp and tears too hot. If you love us like you say you do, you will leave.

Your Daughter.

The pills sit proudly on the table, they call me names, patiently waiting for a reaction, For me to break, *Coward, weak, too scared to even end your suffering,* I swallow back the tears, grab the lump in my throat with my teeth, And throw it to the side, The memories are a movie and I know I will watch, This feels lucid, surreal, Like I am watching myself through a fun house mirror, *I can do this,* I have perfected this moment, Meticulously executed it to the last second, I have done and redone the math, I know what to do, They say in the last moments of one's life, A white light appears, a suffocating peace, Everything I have craved, I don't see the light, Instead, I see the solemn, empty faces of those I have left behind, The tear-streaked pillowcases and shawls, The numb reactions of those I love when they open the letters, I left them, I see dad, finally maybe realizing what he has done to us, I love you still, mama, don't cry. I see Azlan, confused and sad, desperate for me to tell him his angry face is not angry, just cute, one last time, I Azlan shaking me, trying to wake me, The same way he did when we played doctors, I see those seemingly insignificant people sending fake apologies, I see my twenty-five-year-old self, trying to contain her smile as she takes the oath to defend her country from enemies foreign and domestic. The only future I wanted. I'm sorry mama, I love you so,

If I forged a million lies to make you stay, would that be so wrong?

-A

the lie slips from my lips like honey, slick and sweet.

we're playing cat and mouse only he doesn't know it yet, he is a time pass, a soul to be used and abused, is he foolish enough to believe I love him?

he doesn't love me either, he thinks he does, but I know the truth, I'm bored, and he is conveniently around and desperate to love me, his hopes for a family with me rise like the tides, they will drown him.

I have gotten so good at this game, I am an old player, I know there are no rules, I have learnt to change the game if I cannot beat the odds, I will pretend to love him, giving him just enough rope to hang himself,

and when he is crushed and barely breathing, with his heart rolled out onto the grass, bloody with the shame of being unloved and used, I will smile my sweet smile and bury him next to the rest,

-A

My mother used to tell me that I am the kind of girl who will pour water down the drain in front of a dying, thirsty man instead of giving it to him. Of course, I never actually believed her, not completely anyway. But now, some years and an entire lifetime later I finally understand her, finally realize that what she said was true. There is a cruelness in me, a desperate need to even the score, to do anything to those I love if they hurt me, even if it only hurts a little. I do not think I am capable of anything else; I am not forgiving nor empathetic enough to pull the knife out of my back and not stab someone else. Sometimes there is a beauty in being so insensitive, it is like a superpower, a seemingly never-ending high.

Better the devil you know, than the one you don't, as they always say, but what if you're both? Those who really know me, see the flash of liquid rage in my eyes when I'm angry, it lasts a few seconds only, it crashes and then I take it. I swallow the boiling rage and force myself to become the kind and sensitive person mom wishes I were. When all I want to be is quick and sharp and hurtful, it's nature and can we even change that? Can we blame people for the way they're born?

I dream of you so often. My memory cannot forget you, even if I want to. You're burned behind my eyelids, A vivid reality, too far from me, I watch myself sleep, caught between the winds of then and now, I'm floating, hurtling through time yet I can't reach you, you are always just out of reach, have your eyes always been this blue? Every time I look at you is like the first time, I'm still here, waiting, Come home. I loved you some days. But most days I hated you. Most days, I hated you so much that the anger was blistering. Of course, you didn't know that I hated you, if there's anything useful my father taught me, it was how to master self-reinvention. How to pretend. Fake. Shed. Being with you, I changed personalities like clothes. A different one every day. That's how I know that you didn't love me, you couldn't, even when you said you did. You didn't know me; you knew the people I pretended to be. It was your fault, you made me do it. You were so boring, always making demonstrations of your love for me, as if I even cared. You forced me to yell, accuse, gaslight. You forced me to leave you. But not all of it was terrible, sometimes it was silent, like cold, deep water, sometimes it was filtered sunlight, pills and cold coffee. Grandfather clocks, showers and vodka. I hated you most days, but I loved you some too. And sometimes, that alone is enough.

We married each other on a Friday night in my kitchen. We were supposed to marry at three that afternoon but you had connection issues so we couldn't. I thought you'd changed your mind. The decision to marry each other was impulsive, I bathed in impulsivity and you were surprised when I said we should get married. But you are so frantically and childishly in love with me that I could've told you to jump off a bridge and you would've done it, eyes drowned in the foggy sheen that is blinding.

I put my dress on and then took it off. You called too late, and we ended up getting married in pajamas. I don't love you, I could. I could've loved you if I was capable. But every time you're near, I see his steely eyes in your warm brown ones, and I hear his voice in yours. My soul knows this is a mistake. I am lonely and sick with missing him and you are here. A perfectly sweet boy, always pleasing.

My momma doesn't know that I married you. We used post-its and I loved it. I love how you make the loneliness feel light. When we were saying our vows, I was talking to him, not you. You floated out of vision and he was there. Dressed in that navy shirt, the one that crinkled in all the right places. I think I married you to punish him, not that it matters, but it does. Marrying you was like giving him a huge fuck you! It was saying 'I can hurt you too, I am really good at hurting people.'

I married you and yet I didn't. I hate you yet I loved marrying you. I loved how you cried. I loved how you made promises that nobody can ever keep but try anyway.

I am sorry that I have used you, again. I am trying to be better. I'll give our small marriage a real chance. As real as I can. But you have to stop being kind. You have to stop being kind and sweet and loving, it makes it so easy to hurt and use you when you're those things. You're so opposite from him. He was cold and defensive and selfish, something mad and wonderful. But mostly, he was a drug I couldn't stop shooting. You're not a drug, but you're not an antidote either. Stop trying to be an antidote.

AUTHORS NOTE &

ACKNOWLEDGMENTS.

Authors Note: Thank you for following me on this journey through what I have felt. Feelings are a blessing and curse; I realize that now. I understand that I have not always been the victim, but perhaps being the victim for so long, turned me into the perpetrator. I think it's incredibly hard to be anything else other than what you've been taught. I grew up being taught to stab others in the back before they get a chance to stab me. To do to others, before they do to me. That cycle is almost impossible to break, a non-trusting, self-sabotaging game that I always lose. Dad failed to mention that, we're all losers in this game. I am working hard to be everything my father wasn't. I am learning that it doesn't have to be all or nothing, all the time. That I can be sensitive and empathetic and trusting, but sometimes the old me comes back. The sharp, deceitful, hurt me comes out and the simple truth is that sometimes, it's just easier to stay down. It's easier to give in than fight. Someone I used to know once told me that life is hardly sparing. I never truly understood the meaning of that till later on. There is limited room for error in this life. If I could go back in time, I would do things so differently. I would grab my pride by the throat and throw her to the side. I would sweep up the broken glass and glue my heart back together. I wouldn't intentionally break others. I would embrace the sweet, calm traits my mom gave me, instead of calling them weaknesses. I think that this world needs both selfless and selfish to make sense, but that it will always belong to the selfish. I have been a writer at heart for a very long time. Truthfully, I don't know how this collection of poetry and prose came together. All I remember are unbearably hurtful moments and stripping them down to words. And in the midst of all that pain, loss and depression, I created this. The only worthwhile thing birthed by my experiences.

This book would mean nothing if it weren't for all of you readers. You have watched the trailer of a very long movie. Stepped into my shoes and tried to exist. Danced and drank with the devil only to realize that the person you're dancing with, is yourself. To everyone who has grown up in abusive homes, you don't have to stay this way. I know it feels safe and familiar, but it will eat you from the outside in. for those who developed other relationships to feel wanted, safe, it's okay. You don't have to apologize for the ways you tried to numb your pain. This is my truth, speak yours. Always speak yours.

From the bottom of my wretched, empty heart, thank you for allowing me to share my pain so freely.

-Aymen.

Acknowledgments: To J. Walden, thank you for supporting me, making me feel safe and mattered. It has been my privilege to be the recipient of your knowledge and teaching all those years. You add creativity and scope to teaching. Lastly, you have always known the bounds of my potential and given me the space to blossom into it. Thank you to my wonderful psychology teacher, Kate Hammond. Kate, you have taught me so much more than Sperry, Pilliavin, Gottesman and Sazasz. You have seen me, even when I have not. You have given me the confidence, tools and memories that I am certain will fuel my biggest successes. Kate, you have been more than just my teacher, but my friend too. You taught me that I am worthy of asking for help, that I can do whatever I want in this world, I owe you one. Thank you to Sarah Lawton, Caroline Sykes, and Adele Vevers, you have left such a mark on me, a glowing one. Thank you for sharing your knowledge with me, for teaching me to embrace myself, to never be anything less than confident, and to never, ever give up. Thank you to my wonderful parents, yes, even dad. You have given me everything, kept me here, supported me whenever you could. Dad, thank you for doing what you did to us, you have taught me that when someone shows me who they really are, I need to believe them. You have taught me what I want and what I do not. You have given me an entire lifetime of hurt and lessons that I can turn into light. Mom, thank you for always sacrificing yourself for us. I finally understand why you couldn't just up and leave. Thank you to Dr F McCarthy for always fighting for me, for my recovery. To Aroobah and Shery, for keeping me

level and loved. Thank you, Alex, wherever you are. Dead
or alive, I have loved you in every lifetime, Thank you.
Lastly, thank you Azlan, for keeping me bound, for
teaching me to live again, for surprising me with your
words. You are my soulmate, now and forever. I love you
Azlan, you're my favorite kind of magic.

Printed in Great Britain
by Amazon

61770378R00057